TO A SPECIAL TEACHER

Jessica   August
                          27,
                          2005

Thank you !

THOMAS KINKADE

A Teacher's Gift

A Teacher's Gift

THOMAS KINKADE

Andrews McMeel
Publishing

Kansas City

www.thomaskinkade.com

ISBN: 0-7407-4016-4

Library of Congress Catalog Card Number: 2003111245

Compiled by Patrick Regan

Education is
the movement from darkness to light.

Allan Bloom

As a painter, I have long believed in the transforming power of light. Light can do more than simply illuminate a scene, it can bring a static image to life. In much the same way, knowledge gives life to the human mind. We are each born with a limitless capacity for knowledge, but before we can experience all the wonders the world has to offer, a light must first be lit within our minds.

No one does more to bring light to young minds than those who teach. It is not a job for the weak of spirit. Teaching is by turns daunting, draining, frustrating, and exasperating. Yet, dedicated teachers never stop teaching. Perhaps they do so because they understand the profound importance of bringing light to the lives of those they teach. Indeed, the best among them know that their most important job isn't imparting information but nurturing a lifelong desire to learn. In this way, the teacher's work continues to bear fruit long after class is dismissed.

A teacher's greatest gift is a mind unbound by limits—it is, in a very real way, the gift of endless possibility.

This book is a tribute to teachers, those generous and dedicated women and men who bring light to the world, one student at a time.

THOMAS KINKADE

discovery

The art of TEACHING is the art of assisting DISCOVERY.

Pablo Casals

Only
the educated
are free.

Epictetus

$\mathcal{A}$

teacher

AFFECTS

ETERNITY;

he can never

tell where his

INFLUENCE

stops.

Henry Brooks Adams

$\mathcal{T}$hose who

LIVE LIFE for

themselves will

be stuck with

themselves —

and little else.

Thomas Kinkade

Life

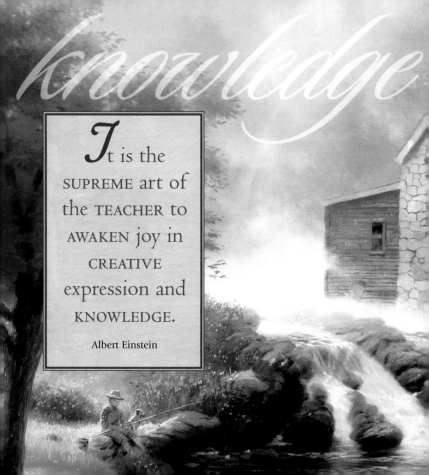

knowledge

$\mathcal{I}$t is the SUPREME art of the TEACHER to AWAKEN joy in CREATIVE expression and KNOWLEDGE.

Albert Einstein

Thomas Kinkade

believe

There is no
real teacher who
in PRACTICE does
not BELIEVE in
the existence of
the SOUL, or in
a MAGIC that
acts on it
through speech.

Allan Bloom

Education

is not

the filling of a pail,

but

the lighting of a fire.

William Butler Yeats

Thomas Kinkade

No one has
yet realized
the WEALTH of
sympathy,
the KINDNESS and
GENEROSITY
hidden in the soul
of a child.
The effort of
every true
EDUCATION should
be to unlock that
TREASURE.

Emma Goldman

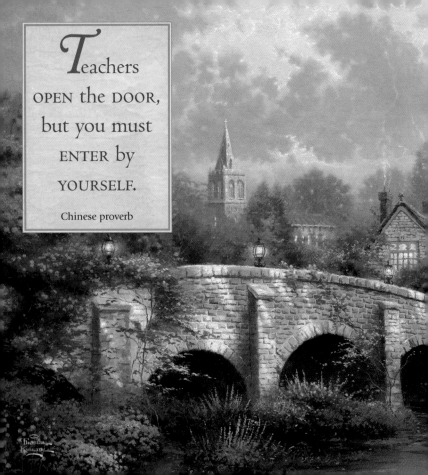

*T*eachers
OPEN the DOOR,
but you must
ENTER by
YOURSELF.

Chinese proverb

Who dares to Teach must never cease to Learn.

John Cotton Dana

My HEART is singing for
the JOY of this morning.
A MIRACLE has happened!
The LIGHT of UNDERSTANDING
has shown upon my little
pupil's MIND, and behold, all
things are CHANGED!

Anne Sullivan

Thomas
Kinkade

$\mathcal{M}$y JOY in LEARNING is partly that it ENABLES me to TEACH.

Seneca

A TEACHER
is one who
MAKES himself
PROGRESSIVELY
unnecessary.

Thomas Carruthers

progress

Thomas Kinkade

*M*an's MIND, once stretched by a new IDEA, never regains its original DIMENSIONS.

Oliver Wendell Holmes, Jr.

EDUCATION has
for its OBJECT the
formation of
CHARACTER.

Herbert Spencer

Thomas Kinkade

*G*ENIUS
without
EDUCATION is
like silver in
the mine.

Benjamin Franklin

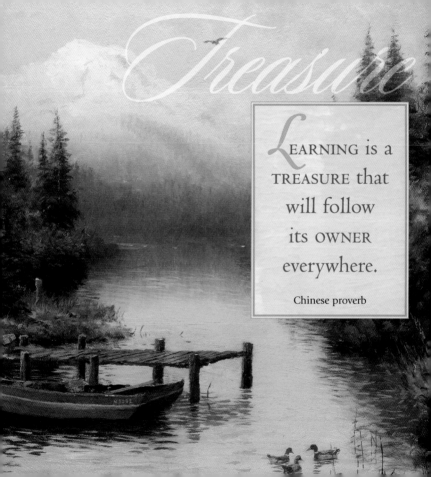

Treasure

LEARNING is a
TREASURE that
will follow
its OWNER
everywhere.

Chinese proverb

We make the BEST
contribution in areas
where our HEARTS call us
TO SERVE — and often
these are areas where we
have either a natural
TALENT or an interest.

Thomas Kinkade

*S*chool

The things TAUGHT in schools and colleges are not an EDUCATION, but the means of EDUCATION.

Ralph Waldo Emerson

*A*n EDUCATION isn't how much you have COMMITTED to MEMORY or even how much you know. It's being ABLE to DIFFERENTIATE between what you know and what you don't.

Anatole France

Thomas Kinkade

The MEDIOCRE
teacher TELLS.
The GOOD
teacher EXPLAINS.
The SUPERIOR
teacher
DEMONSTRATES.
The GREAT
teacher INSPIRES.

William Arthur Ward

By
LEARNING you
will teach; by
TEACHING you
will learn.

Latin proverb

*T*hat is what
LEARNING is.
You suddenly
UNDERSTAND
something you've
understood all
your LIFE, but in
a new way.

Doris Lessing

life

Thomas Kinkade

Education
is
Freedom.

André Gide

The whole art of TEACHING is only the art of AWAKENING the natural CURIOSITY of young minds for the PURPOSE of satisfying it afterward.

Anatole France

*D*elightful task! To rear the TENDER THOUGHT, To TEACH the young IDEA how to shoot.

James Thomson

The DIRECTION in which EDUCATION starts a man will determine his future LIFE.

Plato

A teacher who can arouse a feeling for one single good action, for one single good poem, accomplishes more than he who fills our memory with rows and rows of natural objects, classified with name and form.

Johann Wolfgang von Goethe

accomplish

Imagination

IMAGINATION
is more
important than
KNOWLEDGE.
Knowledge is
limited.
Imagination
encircles the
WORLD.

Albert Einstein

Seek

*I*f you truly want to BLESS others in your life, you must SEEK out those EXPERIENCES that keep you MOTIVATED and INSPIRED, and then SHARE them.

Thomas Kinkade

wisdom

S o teach us
to number our
days, that we
may apply our
hearts unto
wisdom.

Psalms 90:12

Thomas
Kinkade

The brighter you are,

the more you have to

Learn.

Don Herold

EDUCATION
makes a people
easy to LEAD, but
difficult to drive;
easy to GOVERN
but impossible
to enslave.

Baron Henry Peter Brougham

You cannot TEACH a man anything; you can only HELP him find it within himself.

Galileo

$\mathcal{I}$t's a VITAL thing to REMEMBER both as CREATIVE people and those who have the opportunity to NURTURE the creativity in others: Creativity requires COURAGE!

Thomas Kinkade

A
CHILD
cannot be
TAUGHT by
anyone who
despises
him, and a
child cannot
AFFORD to
be fooled.

James Baldwin

$\mathcal{E}$DUCATION is what HAPPENS to the other person, not what comes out of the mouth of the EDUCATOR.

Miles Horton

education

The
Teacher
is one who makes two ideas grow where only one grew before.

Elbert Hubbard

grow

*E*ducation
is not
PREPARATION
for life;
EDUCATION is
life itself.

John Dewey

Thomas
Kinkade

Lead

Choosing to put another's needs above your own doesn't mean ignoring your own NEEDS for rest, for refreshment, for NOURISHMENT. To LEAD an effective LIFE of service, you need to take CARE of yourself.

Thomas Kinkade

*T*O TEACH a
man how he
may LEARN
to GROW
INDEPENDENTLY,
and for
himself, is
perhaps the
GREATEST
service that
one man can
do another.

Benjamin Jowett

Love

We can't form our CHILDREN in our own concepts; we must take them and LOVE them as GOD gives them to us.

Johann Wolfgang von Goethe

virtue

The very spring and ROOT of HONESTY and VIRTUE lie in GOOD education.

Titus Vespasianus

One

Education
is simply the
Soul
of a society
as it passes
from one generation
to another.

G. K. Chesterson

to another

Teaching
is the greatest act of
Optimism.

Colleen Wilcox